THE KLUTZ HANDBOOK

THE KLUTZ HANDBOOK

A Testimonial to Human Nature

Andrew David

ARGUS COMMUNICATIONS
A Division of DLM, Inc.
Allen, Texas 75002

Acknowledgments

Excerpts from *The Incomplete Book of Failures* by Stephen Pile, © Copyright 1979 by Stephen Pile, reprinted by permission of the publisher, E. P. Dutton.

Excerpt from the *1980 Britannica Book of the Year,* © Copyright 1980 by Encyclopaedia Britannica, Inc., Chicago, Illinois, reprinted by permission.

"Special Recognitions" on pages 31 and 48 are reprinted with permission from *Felton and Fowler's Best Worst and Most Unusual,* © Copyright 1975, 1976 by Information House Book, Inc.

"Special Recognition" on page 50 from *The Book of Lists* by David Wallechinsky, Irving Wallace, and Amy Wallace, Copyright 1977, by permission of William Morrow and Co.

Photo/Illustration Credits

The Bettmann Archive   22
The Chicago Tribune Co.   42
Historical Pictures Service   29, 70
Dusty Rumsey   10, 12, 27, 34, 40, 44, 65, 72
Tampa Tribune-Times   54
United Press International   36
Cover Photo by Weems Hutto

FIRST EDITION

© Copyright 1980 Argus Communications, A Division of DLM, Inc.

All rights reserved. No portion of this book may be reproduced, stored in a retrieval system, or transmitted in any form by any means—electronic, mechanical, photocopying, recording, or otherwise—without prior permission of the copyright owner.

Printed in the United States of America.

Argus Communications
A Division of DLM, Inc.
One DLM Park
Allen, Texas 75002

International Standard Book Number: 0-89505-052-8

*For David Scott Taylor
this book is honorarily
and appropriately dedicated.*

Introduction, 9

A Great Tradition, 15

Historically Speaking, 25

The World Around Us, 33

In Sports, 53

Our Way With Words, 67

Coping, 77

Introduction

In every human being there is a little *klutz*.

It would be nice if all of us were perfect, but life doesn't work that way. Fred Astaire has stumbled going up the stairs. Elizabeth Taylor has spilled food on her dress at a gala Hollywood party. The Queen of England has split a royal seam. Others have drunk from their fingerbowls, neglected to zip important zippers, walked into the wrong public rest room, backed their fannies into chairs that weren't there or their convertibles into police cars that were.

The problem is universal. We all mess up. Some folks do it clumsily, others with a great deal of panache, and a few err in such a grand style that their golden moments are remembered for generations.

In this book we will explore some of the ways that people have made klutzes of themselves in the past and investigate the avenues open to ordinary people today who yearn to embarrass themselves in some monumental fashion. This is a book to remind us of our basic faults and foibles and to offer all readers solace by demonstrating that none of us are alone in our moments of ineptitude.

Where do we begin? Perhaps with the word *klutz*, which has been adopted by the multitudes to describe a person who goofs up.

In the past, it has been used to refer to any hapless individual who has acquired a reputation for clumsy and awkward behavior. Clumsiness is not limited to physical movement, however, so we must expand our definition to include those who, through the careful exercise of bad judgment, incomplete investigation of the facts, poor timing, misunderstanding, or simple stupidity, have made fools of themselves or created disaster for those in their vicinity. Further, we will not exclude organizations, companies, and governments from this designation—certainly all such formal bodies have committed whoppers in times past. Here, then, is our working definition of a word that will be used throughout this book:

> klutz/kləts/, *n* 1. a clumsy and awkward person 2. a person who chooses words or courses of action that he shouldn't 3. a person whose words or actions are inherently embarrassing *Syn.:* CLOD, NERD, SCHLEP, SCHLUNK, etc. klutzy, *adj* characterized by clumsiness or foolishness: *as*, That was a really *klutzy* move.

The word *klutz* is known the world over. The crusty New Englander who reaches into a lobster trap without looking inside first is a klutz—sometimes a fingerless klutz. The Californian who builds his house on a mud cliff feels like a klutz after the winter rains. France's famous Inspector Clouseau has filled the bill since the first Pink Panther movie (although in his case it is pronounced "le kloot"). Our trained researchers report that the word is used as far north as the Arctic Circle, usually to characterize Eskimo fishermen who topple into their ice holes. You'll find klutzes in Tokyo, in China, in India, in Africa—and in any other inhabited region; *everyone* screws up from time to time.

Klutzes show their true colors in word and deed. Some unique combinations of the two have also been accomplished under the right circumstances ("You can get your money back by just sticking your hand up the coin return, like this"). Language, however, provides the most numerous and varied opportunities to screw up, probably because we use it incessantly and daily. Besides, all too many of us feel ready to speak up before we really know what's going on. Some examples?

11

"Sure nuclear power is controversial, but you put the plant in some obscure burg like Three Mile Island, Pennsylvania, and no one will ever even know it's there" (Obscure bureaucrat—who undoubtedly will remain obscure).

For World War II buffs: "For the second time in our history, a British Prime Minister has returned from Germany bringing peace with honor. I believe it is peace for our time. . . . Go home and get a nice quiet sleep" (Neville Chamberlain, September 30, 1938).

Even a book editor can do it: "A lot of people are jogging, but don't be ridiculous; *none* of them is going to sit down and read a book about it, much less buy one."

Some people earn their klutz merit badges simply by being in the wrong place at the wrong time—say, in the Holy Land during the Six Day War, for example.

But the good old-fashioned klutz—the clumsy type who causes mayhem in all settings—is still the best source of belly laughs for many of us. Picture this: As guest of honor at a large dinner party hosted by your girlfriend's parents, you are chagrined to discover that your fly is open. Continuing to smile and talk to the person across the table from you, you ever so discreetly zip it up, never realizing that you are securely zipping the tablecloth into your pants. No one notices until just before dessert when you excuse yourself and get up to go into the living room. The china and silverware come with you.

Why all this fuss about moments that most people would like to live down—and forget? Because klutziness is an elemental part of the human condition. It shows up in government, in the military, in sports, in public life. It appears in every arena in which the human animal has distinguished itself at other, brighter times. Often it does us good to remember that we are not infallible, and in chuckling at our foibles we may learn to understand ourselves better while taking ourselves less seriously. As Alexander Pope once wrote: "To err is human." To laugh about it is also human, especially if the error is made by someone else.

A Great Tradition

From the Bible

For centuries, the Bible has been the world's best-selling and most widely read book—an inspiration to millions. But the Bible is also a remarkable source book for the chronicler of human error. Scattered among its wonderful stories and great revelations are countless tales of cues missed, instructions disobeyed, and situations mishandled. An interested reader can find information about some of the earliest blunders in the human saga.

Indeed, the Bible contains an account of the first and most far-reaching instance of human error. Let's set the scene. Adam and Eve are living in bliss in a magnificent garden. They've got it made. If they're hungry, they eat—beautiful fruits and vegetables hang from trees and vines everywhere they look. If they're tired, they sleep. They don't know what pain is, or shame, or loneliness. Apparently, though, Adam and Eve do not find this arrangement satisfactory, and they soon find a way to make some changes. To get things rolling, Eve begins to spend an inordinate amount of time talking to a snake—perhaps students of the animal kingdom conducted interviews in the days before the scalpel and the microscope. Eventually, the creature persuades her to taste the forbidden fruit, and when Adam follows suit, he and his wife are unceremoniously thrown out of Paradise. Mankind loses the garden of felicity—and all for a mere apple. The first couple do not get humanity off on the proverbial right foot.

Food figured significantly in other stories from the old days as well, though nothing quite tops the apple episode. Esau came close when he traded his birthright—a valuable item back then by anyone's standards—to his brother Jacob for a bowl of lentil soup.

Ancient methods of population control must have been more stringent than those employed today. Sovereigns fearful of undesirable elements among the citizenry sometimes organized convenient purges, with infants under the age of two generally being first to go. Lepers didn't last long in a well-run community either; they were driven to isolated areas far from the safety of villages and towns. And animal sacrifice was a routine affair. In sum, it was exceptionally difficult to get along in biblical times if you were a baby, a leper, or a lamb.

Some folks in the Bible were a little slow on the uptake. For instance, when the Egyptian Pharaoh refused Moses' polite suggestion that he free the Hebrews from slavery, all the water in Egypt turned into blood. The frightened Pharaoh agreed to grant Moses his petition, but when the plague was lifted he reneged on his promise. In the face of eight successive plagues—frogs, lice, flies, cattle sickness, body sores, hail, locusts, and darkness—the Pharaoh continued to vacillate, apparently clinging to the groundless conviction that he had the upper hand.

Finally, the plague that wiped out the eldest sons of every family in Egypt convinced the Pharaoh that he was playing with fire, and he allowed the Hebrews to leave his country. Moses neatly parted the waters of the Red Sea to form a dry path by which his people could pass theatrically out of Egypt, but the Egyptian soldiers were not so lucky. Instructed by their commanding officer to pursue their quarry by the Red Sea route, they found that the watery cliffs flanking the path were only temporary.

Then there was the architect who designed the walls of Jericho.

King Solomon's son Rehoboam was a true visionary. When

asked by the people of Israel to cut back on the already exorbitant taxes he had imposed, he set an example that would be followed by rulers and lawmakers for ages thereafter: He *raised* the taxes. Naturally the people revolted, and Rehoboam—whose name, ironically, means "the kingdom shall be enlarged"—lost ten of the twelve tribes of Israel to Jeroboam, a leader of the opposition. Standard-sized champagne bottles are named for the ancient kings. (Interestingly, the big, 3-magnum measure is known as a rehoboam while the smaller size—1.6 magnums—is called a jeroboam.)

The exploits of biblical klutzes are all the more admirable because most of these bunglers had no examples to follow. With luck and originality, they found ways to conduct their lives with striking ineptitude. And the history of klutziness was just beginning.

* * * * *

Special Recognition

"And Absalom met the servants of David. And Absalom rode upon a mule, and the mule went under the thick boughs of a great oak, and his head caught hold of the oak, and he was taken up between the heaven and the earth; and the mule that was under him went away . . .

"And a certain man saw it, and told Joab, and said, Behold, I saw Absalom hanged in an oak . . .

"Then said Joab, I may not tarry thus with thee. And he took three darts in his hand, and thrust them through the heart of Absalom, while he was yet alive in the midst of the oak."

—II Samuel 18

Special Recognition

"And he (Jonah) said unto them, Take me up, and cast me forth into the sea; so the sea shall be calm unto you . . .

"So they took up Jonah and cast him forth into the sea, and the sea ceased from her raging . . .

"Now the Lord had prepared a great fish to swallow up Jonah. And Jonah was in the belly of the fish three days and three nights."

—Jonah 1

Special Recognition

"And it came to pass, when they had brought them forth abroad, that he said, Escape for thy life; look not behind thee . . .

"Then the Lord rained upon Sodom and upon Gomorrah brimstone and fire from the Lord out of heaven . . .

"But his (Lot's) wife looked back from behind him, and she became a pillar of salt."

—Genesis 19

From the Ancients

The average ancient was a lot like us. Romans managed to trip over their togas and Etruscans broke a lot of their fancy vases. Pompeiians built their city at the foot of an active volcano, the people of Crete occasionally got tangled up in their own fishing nets, and there is little doubt that some now-forgotten Carthaginian fell victim to the enormous feet of an elephant in Hannibal's army.

Even the so-called great thinkers of those days got into the act. The Roman astronomer Ptolemy, esteemed throughout the ancient world, provided an authoritative (and totally erroneous) picture of the solar system when he declared that the sun revolved around the earth and that the earth itself was an absolutely immovable object. Nobody had any better ideas until Copernicus came along 1,400 years later. Aristotle insisted that heavier objects fall faster than light ones, that the air helps move objects that are thrown through it, that celestial bodies are made of a mysterious substance called *ether*, and that physical feelings and sensations are generated in the heart rather than in the brain. Socrates was known to stand totally enraptured without moving a muscle for periods as long as twenty-four hours, sometimes even in the rain. Fortunately for these sages and others like them, it would be centuries before anyone recognized the foolishness of some of their crackpot theories.

When the emperor Nero ascended the Roman throne as a teenager, he decided that life would be less complicated if his mother, Agrippina, were not around to hound him about things. But the young emperor did not deal with the situation very effectively. First he tried poison—but Agrippina was immune. She was on to that kind of trick because she had employed it against her late husband, the emperor Claudius I. One night soon after the failure of his first plan, Nero arranged for the heavy stone ceiling in Agrippina's chamber to come crashing down upon her bed—but she left the room moments before the "accident." Next, Nero sent a sailing ship to bring his mother to an island where he said they could work out their differences together. The ship he sent was designed to break apart on the high seas, and it did—but Agrippina managed to swim safely to shore. Finally, Nero abandoned his klutzy death plots and simply ordered his mother's execution. A band of legionnaires carried out the emperor's command with impressive dispatch at Agrippina's country home.

* * * * *

Human beings, however extraordinary or prophetic they might have been, weren't the only creatures messing things up in the early days of civilization. The Babylonians, the Chaldeans, the Celts, and other ancient peoples told stories of strange happenings in the heavens. In the western world we are most familiar with the exploits of Greek and Roman gods and heros. The ancient stories are interesting because they portray gods and goddesses who fall prey to the same follies that guided humans then (and guide them now) into sticky or embarrassing situations.

For instance, Cupid, the god of love, was an archer of extraordinary merit, but he once wounded himself with one of his own arrows. Pandora, like Eve, found the word *no* an irresistible incitement to action. She insisted on disobeying her husband, Epimetheus, by opening the famous forbidden box, thereby letting into the world many of the evils that afflict humanity even today. A shipwrecked mariner named Ajax the Less owed his life to the sea god, Poseidon. Before the waves could carry away the hapless sailor, Poseidon cast him safely onto a rock jutting from the raging sea. But instead of graciously thanking his benefactor, Ajax bragged that he had saved himself. The irritated Poseidon split the rock in two, allowing Ajax to fall into the sea and drown.

* * * * *

Parents of teenagers who want to use the family car should take note of the story of Phaethon, son of a mortal woman and the sun-god, Phoebus. Phaethon wanted to drive his father's great four-horse sun-chariot across the sky. He badgered and pestered and pleaded, ignoring his father's warning that only a strong man could safely direct the spirited steeds. Phaethon was adamant, and finally his father gave in. As you might have guessed, the boy soon lost control of the fiery chariot. It plummeted toward earth, burning cities and scorching plains as it dipped ever closer to the ground. When Zeus realized that the chariot would set the whole world on fire if it crashed, he blew up both chariot and rider with a well-aimed thunderbolt. (Phaethon's body, incidentally, fell into the river Po and his sisters queued up along the bank to weep for him. For some reason known only to Zeus, they were turned into poplar trees.)

Like Phaethon, Icarus wanted to soar across the heavens, and like Phaethon, he wasn't too smart. When he rose high above the trees, the sun melted the wax that held together his homemade wings. He fell into the sea and was drowned.

GIFT HORSE DEPARTMENT

The Trojan War pitted the Greek and Trojan armies against each other for nine long years. Both sides lost many heroes in the battle, but finally the invading Greeks decided to take the city of Troy by stratagem. They built an enormous wooden horse, hollow on the inside and capable of concealing a great number of warriors. Leaving it unattended outside the walls of Troy, they pretended to depart in their ships after circulating the rumor that the horse was a Greek offering to Athena which would lose its efficacy if brought inside the walls of Troy. Naturally, plenty of savvy Trojans rose to the occasion: "Hey, look at the great wooden horse the Greeks brought for us. Bring it inside so we can all see it." And thus Troy lost the war.

The fall of Icarus.

Special Recognition

Long before malpractice suits became popular, Xenophon, a physician in Rome during the first century A.D., was called upon to attend the gravely ill emperor Claudius I. The emperor's wife, Agrippina, had been feeding him poisoned mushrooms. Xenophon quickly diagnosed the problem and decided to induce vomiting. He pulled a feather from his medical bag and pushed it down Claudius' throat. The emperor thereupon choked and died.

Special Recognition

In the tales of the ancients, gods and goddesses often made undesirable changes in the shapes of those who displeased them. Occasionally, individuals tried to thwart this intention, but they were seldom successful. For example:

	Boner	*Turned Into*
Alectyron	On assignment to watch for the dawn, he fell asleep.	A cock, doomed forever to wake and crow at dawn.

Andvari	This Norse dwarf turned himself into a pike to avoid his enemy, Loki. Loki decided to go fishing that day.	
Atlas	Refused to extend a welcome to Perseus, a hero who deserved one.	A stone, condemned to support the world on his shoulders eternally.
Charybdis	Stole Hercules' oxen (Hercules was the strongest man on earth.)	A whirlpool.
Children of Ler	Aroused the jealousy of their mother, Aeife.	Swans, doomed to wander the lakes of Ireland for 900 years.*
Io	Aroused the jealousy of Hera.	A cow continually tormented by a gadfly.
Scylla	Was indifferent to the love of the sea-god Glaucus.	A monster.

---

*St. Patrick allegedly restored them to human form and converted them to Christianity, but they were so old by then that they died almost immediately thereafter.

Historically Speaking—
A Klutz Time-line

As Time Goes By

Purists might desire a historical catalogue of all the important bloopers made by governments, leaders of state, military and public figures over the years, but of course this is impossible. Therefore, we have decided to select just a few examples and to offer them in the form of a time-line. This will help provide a certain continuity to our chronicle of klutzdom. Unfortunately, we must skip the Dark Ages; those 1,000 years provide too rich a bounty of idiocy for us to select a representative sampling. For example, Attila the Hun, a stellar personage of the period, encouraged his soldiers to drink the blood of their horses. The Teutons burned virgins as battle sacrifices . . . I rest my case.

Somewhere around the year 1500, men and women began to approach life with a little more sense, a better touch on reality, with certain cultivated values and moral sense. In those days, developments in society, the sciences, and culture were preparing the way for people like Copernicus, Galileo, Newton, Darwin, Einstein, and all the modern philosophers and poets and scientists. They were opening the door to a variety of other things as well. For example:

***Approximately
or specifically,
as the case
may be***

1513 The Spanish government funds Juan Ponce de Leon to seek out the Fountain of Youth, allegedly bubbling on the island of Bimini. Instead he discovers Florida.

1557 The papacy introduces the Roman Catholic Index of Prohibited Books. It will eventually include most or all the major works of such writers as Boccaccio, Galileo, Francis Bacon, Thomas Hobbes, Rene Descartes, John Milton, John Locke, Daniel Defoe, Immanuel Kant, Oliver Goldsmith, Casanova, Edward Gibbon, Alexandre Dumas (*pere* and *fils*), George Sand, Victor Hugo, Gustave Flaubert, and Emile Zola, among others.

1588 King Philip II of Spain sends his famous "invincible" Armada to fight the English navy, effectively ruining the fleet's record.

1626 Peter Minuit buys Manhattan Island from the Man-a-Hat-a Indians for trinkets valued at $24.00. (These days, most people agree that Peter Minuit was the one taken in the deal.)

1633 The Court of the Inquisition forces Galileo to publicly recant his teachings, drawn from scientific evidence, that the earth does indeed revolve around the sun.

1639 The first act of Prohibition is introduced in the United States (in Massachusetts).

1692 Massachusetts does it again. Thirty-one individuals (twenty-five women, six men) are tried and convicted of being witches. The death penalty is carried out in twenty cases—nineteen "witches" are hanged, and one is slowly crushed to death beneath a pile of rocks.

1775 On his way to inform the citizens of Concord, New Hampshire, that the British are coming, Paul Revere is arrested by the Redcoats and his horse is confiscated.

1775 In the heat of the American Revolutionary War, Colonel Ethan Allen—frontiersman, soldier, and Green Mountain Boy—attacks the city of Montreal, for some reason. He is captured by the bewildered and angry Canadians.

1784 Benjamin Franklin nominates the turkey for the position of honor as national bird of the United States.

1797 Senator William Blount of Tennessee incites the Creek and Cherokee Indians to revolt against the king of Spain, triggering the first trial on impeachment charges in the U.S. Senate. The charges were dismissed eventually, but Blount was kicked out of the Senate anyway.

1804 Alexander Hamilton agrees to settle his differences with Aaron Burr in a duel at Weehawken, New Jersey.

1830 William Huskisson, a member of Parliament in London, becomes the first person in history to be run over by a railroad train. At the opening ceremonies of the Manchester and Liverpool Railway, he decides to cross the tracks to speak with the Duke of Wellington and is hit by the train.

1841 William Henry Harrison refuses to wear a hat at his outdoor inauguration ceremonies, even though it is raining. He catches cold and dies, becoming the first U.S. president to die in office.

1857 The U.S. Army Camel Corps is formally conscripted, with seventy-five camels imported from North Africa. They do not prove to be a boon to the U.S. cavalry because, according to one historian: "The strange appearance of the camels, their tinkling bells and unfamiliar odor, caused the horses and mules to go berserk."

1864 General Ulysses S. Grant is given command of the Union Army and he immediately institutes an entirely new program of military tactics. During the first month, 60,000 Union soldiers die.

1876 In Montana, scouts for George Armstrong Custer report that they have sighted only a small band of Indians in the area. Custer suggests that the hill above the Little Bighorn River would be as good a place as any to camp.

1883 The first shares in New York City's newly opened Brooklyn Bridge are bought by an out-of-towner.

1890 In an effort to modernize his methods of execution, Emperor Menelik of Abyssinia (today Ethiopia) orders three electric chairs from an American manufacturer of such items. The chairs arrive but do not work—there is no electricity in

The U.S. Camel Corps makes its way across Nevada.

Abyssinia at the time. The emperor makes the best of it, adopting one of them to serve as his official throne.

1914 U.S. Secretary of State William Jennings Bryan invites the Swiss navy to participate in ceremonies officially opening the Panama canal. Swiss officials inform him that Switzerland does not have a navy and has little need for one since the country is entirely landlocked.

1920 The Volstead Act becomes law, and the era of bootleg whiskey, homemade beer, bathtub gin, and the speakeasy is launched.

1921 Warren G. Harding is elected president of the United States.

1957 Ford Motor Company introduces the Edsel.

1958 The United States Air Force accidentally drops a hydrogen bomb into the ocean off the coast of Savannah, Georgia.

1958 The United States Air Force accidentally drops a nuclear bomb on the town of Mars Bluff, South Carolina.

1960 An American U-2 spy plane flown by Francis Gary Powers is shot down over Sverdlovsk, USSR. The U.S. claims that Powers was flying a "weather-research aircraft." The USSR announces that they have the pilot in custody and that the airplane is still intact. The U.S. concedes that the operations for which the plane was used could be described as "spying."

1962 Billy Sol Estes sells fertilizer tanks that do not exist to a variety of investors.

1963 President Lyndon B. Johnson unveils the scar from his gall bladder surgery to the media.

1968 Quote: "I do not believe Hanoi can hold up under a long war."—General William C. Westmoreland.

Quote: "The enemy has lost whatever chance he had of taking South Vietnam by military force." —General Earle G. Wheeler.

Quote: "Truth will become the hallmark of the Nixon Administration." —White House Communications Director Herbert Klein.

1969 Norman Mailer runs for mayor of New York under the slogan "No More Bullshit!" Out of five candidates, he comes in fourth.

1970 The U.S. Air Force holds a formal ceremony at Charleston Air Force Base to introduce the new C-5 transport plane. Officials and guests watch its first operational flight. As it comes in for a landing, one wheel blows out and another comes off and rolls down the runway beside the plane.

1971 McGraw-Hill publishing company gives author Clifford Irving a $100,000 advance against royalties for his work on the "official" biography of Howard Hughes. Mr. Hughes's staff later denies all knowledge of the book.

1972 Watergate: The first attempt—E. Howard Hunt and Virgilio Gonzales are forced to spend the night hiding on a staircase in the Watergate complex when they are unable to open the

door to Democratic National Headquarters.
The second attempt—Gonzales is unable to pick the lock to the headquarters.
The third attempt—The burglars finally get it right, and stage perhaps the biggest political scandal in the nation's history.

1972 The United States Air Force admits that the C-5 transport plane has certain defects, including "engines which tend to fall off (and) . . . wings and landing gear that tend to malfunction."

1974 President Gerald Ford pardons former president Richard M. Nixon.

1979 At the nuclear power reactor at Three Mile Island, Pennsylvania, a series of breakdowns leads to the announcements that a nuclear core meltdown is imminent and a mammoth hydrogen explosion is possible. Immediately thereafter officials assure the media that there is nothing "serious" to worry about.

Special Recognition

Worst Intelligence Report

The English of King Harold's day wore their hair cut about shoulder length, and only the priests had shorter locks. Receiving reports that a party of Normans had landed on English soil, Harold sent out a spy to estimate their numbers and the potential threat they posed. When the secret agent observed a thousand close-cropped Norman soldiers, he mistakenly reported to the king that the French had sent an army of priests across the Channel to "chant masses." This miscalculation of William the Conqueror's forces was one factor contributing to Harold's defeat at Hastings.

The World Around Us

Inside most of us there's a nasty little demon that delights in the blunders of people who have made it to the top. Television, the movies, national magazines, and the gossip columns picture a fairy-tale world peopled by celebrities who seem oblivious to the mundane worries that afflict the rest of us. The average person begins to feel a bit inferior. But retouched photographs, lilting printed descriptions, or self-assurance on television don't tell the whole story about people in high places. And because of media hype, we often feel a devious and strangely comforting malice when we learn that some celebrity has done something really stupid—something we might have done ourselves.

STRANGE BEDFELLOWS DEPARTMENT

Returning home after attending the funeral of Korean president Park Chung Hee in Seoul, Senator S. I. Hayakawa of California dozes in an upper bunk aboard a plane making the long flight back to Washington, D.C. Suddenly, Hayakawa rolls out of his bunk and lands on top of Secretary of State Cyrus Vance's startled security officer. After this impromptu meeting, the senator decides to heed nature's call, since he is down in the aisle of the airplane now

anyway. While he is in the men's room, a stewardess patrolling the aisle notices his unoccupied bunk and slams it shut. A few minutes later Senator Hayakawa retraces his steps, moving down the darkened aisle until he judges that he has reached his bunk. He climbs up the ladder and begins to settle himself comfortably under the covers. This bunk is more crowded than the one he left, though; it is already occupied by President Carter's son Chip.

* * * * *

Some mistakes have much graver consequences. One day in St. Petersburg, Russian composer Peter Ilich Tchaikovsky told his brother he was thirsty and went to fetch himself a glass of water. His brother warned him not to drink the water without boiling it; a cholera epidemic was being spread through the city's water system. Tchaikovsky said "Bosh," or the Russian equivalent, quenched his thirst, and died of cholera shortly thereafter.

BUY AMERICAN DEPARTMENT

In 1927, famous American dancer Isadora Duncan was in Nice, France, considering the purchase of a Bugatti automobile. She took it for a test drive with the top down, her long scarf fluttering in the Mediterranean breeze until it got caught up in the spokes of one of the rear wheels and strangled her to death.

* * * * *

Although voters might question the political competence of some individuals elected to our country's highest office, the roster of United States presidents is filled with names of men who have at least helped to keep the American public amused. Gerald Ford's clumsiness was notorious: bumping his head on an airplane doorway, falling down a flight of stairs, hitting a golf ball into a crowd of spectators, adroitly driving a tennis ball into the back of his doubles partner's head, spilling things on his Oval Office desk. Recording

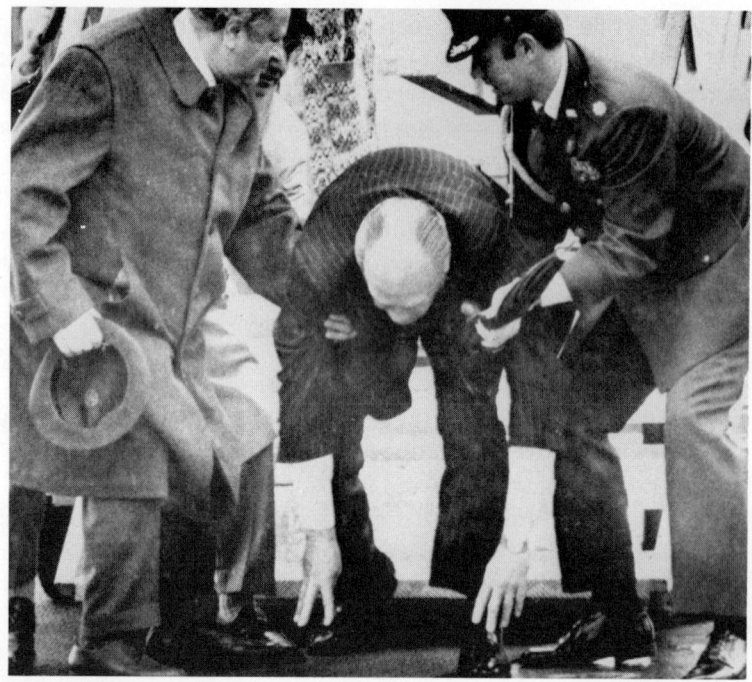

President Gerald Ford demonstrates just a few of the opportunities open to the average klutz by inadvertently assaulting a spectator with a golf ball, cleverly pounding a helicopter with the crown of his head, and ingeniously descending an airplane ramp without using the handrails.

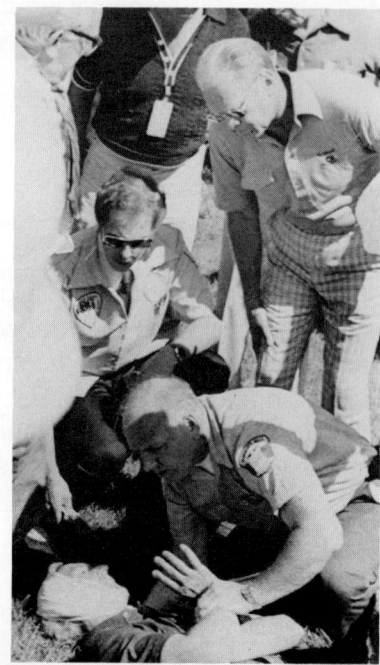

Ford's exploits became a sort of national pastime during his short tenure in office. Interestingly, Ford was the most accomplished athlete ever to hold the presidency, which probably proves that you don't have to be uncoordinated to be clumsy.

One of Jimmy Carter's fishing trips in Plains, Georgia, was marred by the appearance of a vicious rabbit which, according to the president, swam out to his boat to attack him.

Although many a past president has been the butt of unkind jokes, Calvin Coolidge holds the unofficial crown; his years in office were salad days for wits and humorists. An austere, sober-faced, serious man, he was so unanimated that when Dorothy Parker was informed of his death she responded, "How could they tell?"

Red Grange, the great halfback for the Chicago Bears, remembers meeting the president at the White House back in the 1920s. A senator introduced him as "Red Grange, who plays with the Bears." President Coolidge nodded sagely, patted Grange on the shoulder, and confided, "Young man, I always have liked animal acts."

Coolidge's chief of staff liked to recall one day when he met with the president in his White House office to deliver a briefing on some business of state. Time passed, and Coolidge began to nod off; he was asleep before his adviser had finished speaking. Suddenly the president awoke with a start, his eyes focusing on his chief of staff as he asked quickly, "Is the country still here?"

CLOSE SHAVES DEPARTMENT

Although she often delighted in exposing the gaffes of others, Dorothy Parker occasionally slipped up herself. One day during her tenure as a screenwriter in Hollywood, Miss Parker was visited in her office by Mrs. Peabody, the wife of an important studio executive. The Peabodys were hosting a dinner party in a month or so, and Mrs. Peabody had stopped to deliver a personal invitation. Miss Parker did not want to go, but since she did not want to offend those who paid her salary, she said she would be delighted to attend. As soon as her visitor left, Dorothy Parker summoned her secretary and said, far too loudly, "Remind me in a week or so to write those illiterate, phony boors that I can't attend their damned party because . . ." Mrs. Peabody hadn't left, though, and suddenly she appeared, ashen-faced in the doorway to Miss Parker's office. Dorothy Parker paused hardly more than a moment before continuing, "... because I am dining that evening with the Peabodys."

SAY IT WITH FLOWERS DEPARTMENT

George Jessel was scheduled to entertain one evening at a Veterans Administration hospital. When informed that patients and staff alike were looking forward to his show, Jessel asked how many nurses there were on the staff and gallantly ordered an orchid corsage for each of them. When he arrived at the hospital for the show he was greeted by fifty-two male nurses, each sporting an elegant corsage.

BUDDY, CAN YOU SPARE A DIME? DEPARTMENT

John Dewey, the famous American philosopher and educator, was walking with a friend one day across the campus of the university at which he taught when a little boy rushed up and asked him for a nickel. Professor Dewey dug into his pocket for a coin and gave it to the child. Turning to his companion he remarked, "The trouble with the young people of today is they're always asking for money. They just come up out of nowhere and ask anybody on the street." His colleague was silent for a moment. "But that was your son, wasn't it?" Dewey stopped walking as he thought it over. "Well, yes, I guess maybe it was."

* * * * *

Adlai Stevenson, the Democratic candidate for president in 1952, made a tactical error when he preempted the "I Love Lucy" show, which was then at the height of its popularity, to air a campaign message. Later estimates suggest that he may have lost tens of thousands of votes as a result of the unpopular decision. He received thousands of irate letters, most of them not as terse as this one but similar in spirit:

>Dear Mr. Stevenson:
>I love Lucy. I like Ike. Drop dead.

* * * * *

In Mexico City in 1975, orchestra conductor Jose Seribrier got so carried away during a concert that he stabbed himself through the hand with his baton. Undaunted, and with the baton thus impaled, he continued directing the orchestra until a lull in the music afforded him a moment or two to remove the baton from his palm.

* * * * *

Comedian Alan King once performed in London at a show attended by Queen Elizabeth. He was to be formally presented to the queen after the show. A little nervous about meeting such a lofty member of royalty, King had practiced his greeting assiduously: "How do you do, your majesty? . . . How do you do, your majesty?" When he finally stood before her, the queen smiled with dignity and said, "How do you do, Mr. King?" With an attempt at equal dignity, he responded, "How do you do, Mrs. Queen?"

* * * * *

MAKE HAY WHILE THE SUN SHINES DEPARTMENT

The Phoenix Foundation was a sometime real estate company, tax shelter, and even kingdom founder. In 1972, company officials located a lovely coral reef in the South Pacific. Eagerly they staked a claim, planted flags, and declared that the reef was the new republic of Minerva. Unfortunately, the company was unable to fully develop the resources of its new principality. Officials had discovered the reef at low tide, and twelve hours later the republic of Minerva was submerged beneath four feet of water.

* * * * *

We need not look to Hollywood studios, the mansions of Beverly Hills, the White House, or royal palaces for examples of

IT'S DOWN THERE...
NEW REPUBLIC OF MINERVA
P
PHOENIX FOUNDATION

humanity's ineptitude. There are plenty of golden moments to cherish closer to home. They occur daily—hourly, in fact—and members of every profession participate. Consider this uplifting story of those who serve and protect us, excerpted here from *The Book of Heroic Failures*, by Steven Pile.

"The fireman's strike of 1978 made possible one of the great animal rescue attempts of all time. Valiantly, the British army had taken over emergency firefighting and on 14 January they were called out by an elderly lady in South London to retrieve her cat which had become trapped up a tree. They arrived with impressive haste and soon discharged their duty. So grateful was the lady that she invited them all in for tea. Driving off later, with fond farewells completed, they ran over the cat and killed it."

Police work has its own hazards. In 1976, a Chicago police sergeant was walking through the doorway into his commander's office, his hands laden with paperwork, when the hammer of his revolver caught on the door latch, pulling the trigger and sending a bullet coursing down his left leg. He was listed as having shot himself in the line of duty.

The bad guys do not fare much better. A Chicago man's ill-fated attempt to hold up a savings and loan association was described by police in detail:

> "The would-be robber walked up to a teller's window and handed the woman a note that said: 'This is a holdup. Put all the money you have on the counter.'
>
> "He kept one hand inside his coat, as if he had a gun. The teller obeyed his order, stacking $2,845 on the counter. But (the robber) told her: 'That's not enough. How about the coins?'
>
> "When she returned with the bag, the cash was still on the counter, but the holdup man wasn't anywhere to be seen. He had swooned and was lying on the floor out of her sight. Another teller who saw the man—thinking he was a customer—dialed (the emergency telephone number) and asked for an ambulance and an inhalator.

The Chicago Police Department discovers a new way to fight crime on the lakefront by dispatching an amphibious patrol car.

"By the time members of the fire department and police department arrived on the scene, the robber had begun to open his eyes, just in time to be arrested."

Another unskilled robber's plight is of equal interest. He entered a jewelry store on Long Island and pointed a gun at the wide-eyed clerk, who stared not only at the barrel of the gun but at the immensity of the 350-pound man wielding it. The clerk moved along behind the counter emptying the cases as he had been instructed. The robber kept pace until, stumbling, he fell and his gun skittered away from him. He lay helplessly on his back like an enormous upturned turtle, and despite his efforts he could not get up. The relieved clerk called police, who got the bandit to his feet and into a patrol wagon for the trip down to the station house.

* * * * *

Physicians have always been among the most revered of professionals. But as the ever-burgeoning crop of malpractice suits so amply illustrates, there have been plenty of medical blunders in recent years, ranging from the doctor whose scalpel slipped during a routine minor operation, totally severing the operatee's penis, to the nurse-and-doctor team who efficiently rolled a surgical cart—with the patient on it—into an elevator shaft.

Sometimes doctors and hospital staffers just get confused. For example, at a Philadelphia hospital in early 1980, two women were scheduled for surgery on the same day, one to have her parathyroid gland removed and the other to have a ruptured spinal disk repaired. The operations took place in due course. The woman with the bad back left the hospital minus her parathyroid gland and doctors "repaired" a disk in the back of the woman with gland problems. Hospital officials called the mix-up a "million-to-one occurrence" and referred all questions about the incident to their lawyers.

Million to one? Maybe, but less than three months later a young boy in O'Fallon, Illinois, entered the hospital to have his tonsils and adenoids removed. The surgeon enlarged the end of the child's

LOS ANGELES, LOS ANGELES.... THIS IS CORRIGAN FROM NEW YORK... DO YOU READ ME?
...LOUD AND CLEAR CORRY! BUT I'M AFRAID I'VE GOT A BIT OF A SURPRISE FOR YOU, LAD....

urinary tract. The little boy scheduled for the aforementioned operation went home without his tonsils and adenoids.

* * * * *

This item appeared in the *Encyclopaedia Britannica Yearbook, 1980*:

"A Soviet newspaper reported the case of V. I. Matveyev, who entered the hospital to have an artificial joint implanted in a left toe. When Matveyev awoke from surgery, his right foot was bandaged but not his left. He also had a bandage on his right hand. When Matveyev demanded an explanation, the surgeon became irate and wanted to know if Matveyev thought he was smarter than the doctor. As to the hand, it had an unpleasant scar that was removed. The doctor told Matveyev to stop complaining and go back to work after buying a pair of shoes three sizes larger than usual. The matter was taken to local authorities who suspended the doctor's license for three months and warned him to lay off the vodka on the eve of operations."

* * * * *

Airplane pilots have been known to land their aircrafts at the wrong airports, some even allowing their passengers to disembark before learning of the mistake. Granted, it might be disconcerting to step off a plane and into the Pittsburgh air terminal when your destination was Cleveland, but one commercial pilot of yore has all competitors beat in the creative navigational sweepstakes. In the 1930s, Wrong Way Corrigan set out for Los Angeles from New York and flew across the Atlantic, landing instead in Dublin.

An unseasoned pilot in Springfield, Ohio, offered a new one in the annals of aviation mishaps. As he sped down the runway at the throttle of his Mooney M-20F, his flight instructor gave him the usual banter—tips, reminders of operating procedure, and so on. It was important not to wait too long before retracting the landing gear, the instructor said. His apt student took him at his word and performed the operation flawlessly. Unfortunately, the plane had not yet left the runway.

* * * * *

A squadron of Finnish paratroopers once engaged in a war game with an exciting twist. Under their billowy parachutes, they floated down over the drop zone, shed their silks, located the enemy force on the side of a hill, and opened fire (with blanks, of course). Unfortunately, the paratroopers had not located their designated adversaries; the "enemy" they fired upon was a party of hunters who were so startled and frightened by the sudden attack that they began firing back. Fortunately no one was injured; the Finnish paratroopers quickly surrendered when real shotgun pellets began raining down on them.

* * * * *

One evening in 1979, officials informed the family of a Maywood, Illinois, young man that they might be the closest living relatives of a murder victim whose body was being held at the Cook County morgue. The young man's father, his mother, a brother, and his stepfather went to the morgue to identify the corpse. One by one they viewed the body, reluctantly agreeing that police had made a correct identification. Sadly, the group returned home. A few hours later their bereavement was interrupted when the young man they had identified as dead walked in the front door, returning home from a party he had been attending that night.

* * * * *

NOW I LAY ME DOWN TO SLEEP DEPARTMENT

Relationships between men and women are complex, and situations that arise when a couple is together are often embarrassing. The exploits of one young man in British Columbia were reported by newspapers as an excellent application of Murphy's Law, which states that if something can go wrong, it will. On a warm May night in 1980, the young man in question visited his girlfriend at her apartment. He was sitting on her bed (it was a Murphy bed, the kind that folds up into a wall) when suddenly it bolted back up into the wall closet. He found himself upside down with his head stuck in the bed's assembly. When our hero's girlfriend had tried in vain to budge either the bed or its victim she called the police, who were able to free him when they arrived.

LOVE IS A MANY-SPLENDORED THING DEPARTMENT

Chicago radio personality Norman Mark and newspaper columnist Bob Herguth once collected a number of unusual marriage proposals for the public's edification. If you are given to tradition, you might find these a little strange—but variety is the spice of life, as they say.

- Paula and her boyfriend were sitting in his living room. Suddenly he looked over at his pet cockatoo and inquired sweetly, "Muffy, do you want a new Mommy?"
- Steve led his girlfriend into the powder room during a New Year's Eve party, reached behind the dirty clothes hamper, and produced an engagement ring.
- Shirley and her boyfriend were at a family party with a lot of relatives. When Shirley turned away for a moment, her boyfriend dropped an engagement ring into her champagne. She almost choked at the next sip, but managed to retrieve the ring from her mouth and put it on her finger, thus becoming betrothed.
- Bruce was perhaps least bound by the strictures of tradition. He took his girlfriend to a swimming pool, threw her in, leaped in after her, and pulled down his pants to reveal the words printed on his derriere: *Marry Me.*

All of that kind of thing can lead to the altar, of course. But occasionally, things go wrong at the last minute. A young man in Sheffield, England, had to pick up the wedding cake on his way home from a stag party in his honor. He didn't forget, but he dropped it in his fiancee's front yard. The fragile tiers, the baker's carefully wrought flowers and doves and leaves, were instantly transformed into a huge, dripping, white pile of mush. The wedding guests all came outside when they heard the groom cursing the blob at his feet. The bride-to-be's mother was justifiably furious and said so in no uncertain terms. The young man responded with a sharp right to her jaw, knocking her down on top of the onetime cake. His fiancee called the wedding off, explaining later to her guests, "If he had hit me instead of my mother, I probably would have married him all the same, but I'm not having any man hitting my mum."

Special Recognition

In 1971, Hans and Erna W., a Swiss couple vacationing in Hong Kong, stopped to eat at a restaurant there and asked the headwaiter to take their pet poodle, Rosa, into the kitchen and find it something to eat. The waiter misunderstood their request, however, and the couple was aghast when Rosa was brought to their table done to a turn in a round-bottomed frying pan, marinated in sweet-and-sour sauce, and garnished with Chinese vegetables. The meal was left uneaten and the couple were treated for shock.

Special Recognition

We honor here the U. S. government and the various independent foundations responsible for funding these projects or studies:

The average amount of time it takes to cook breakfast—funded by the Department of Agriculture ($46,000)

"The Peruvian Brothel: A Sexual Dispensary and Social Arena"—part of a study funded by the National Institute of Mental Health ($97,000)

What burning paper looks like in the sky—funded by the National Endowment for the Arts ($6,025)

Why prisoners want to escape from jail—funded by the Law Enforcement Assistance Administration ($27,000)

Why people fall in love—funded by the National Science Foundation ($84,000)

Preparation of a dictionary in Tzotzil, an unwritten Mayan language spoken by 12,000 peasants in southern Mexico—funded by the Smithsonian Institution ($89,000)

The attitudes of people playing tennis on public tennis courts—a study funded by the National Endowment for the Humanities ($2,500)

A door-to-door survey of the number of dogs, cats, and horses in or around the houses and apartments in Ventura County, California—funded by the Department of Labor ($384,948)

Our appreciation to Senator William Proxmire of Wisconsin for bringing these to the attention of the public through publication in the Congressional Record. They are only a few of the projects considered for the senator's now famous Golden Fleece of the Month awards, designed, in his words, "to expose the most outrageous example(s) of federal waste." The entire subject is examined in detail in his book *The Fleecing of America* (Houghton Mifflin Company, Boston: 1980).

Special Recognition

Four of the Worst Generals in Recent Military History

Gen. William H. Winder (1775-1824)

In the War of 1812, the American general Winder proved his incompetence with disastrous consequences. In 1813, he lost the battle of Stony Creek even though he had three times as many men as the British. He was captured but, unfortunately for the Americans, the British released him. In 1814, he commanded the American forces protecting Washington, D. C., against the invading British. One charge routed Winder's army, and he fled for safety. The British proceeded to the American capital and burned it.

Gen. Antonio Lopez de Santa Anna (1795?-1876)

The Mexican general Santa Anna, who considered himself the Napoleon of the Americas, lost two wars for Mexico. In 1836, in the Texas War, Santa Anna wasted men and time storming the Alamo. Then he marched north and encamped his army at the San Jacinto River—unaware that a Texan army was only a few miles away. The Texans attacked while Santa Anna and his men were taking their siestas. The Mexican army was destroyed and Santa Anna was captured. In the Mexican-American War (1846-1848), Santa Anna lost every battle he fought.

Gen. Ambrose Burnside (1824-1881)

The Union general Burnside's blunders were innumerable. At the battle of Antietam (1862), he sent masses of men across a narrow bridge where Confederate gunners slaughtered them. If Burnside had reconnoitered, he would have discovered that the river beneath the bridge was only waist deep, and his men could have forded it anywhere, thus avoiding the deadly bridge. At Fredericksburg (1862), Burnside ordered a hopeless, suicidal attack which left 1,284 Union soldiers dead. At the siege of Petersburg (1865), he had a tunnel dug beneath the enemy trenches and filled it with explosives. The powder was detonated, leaving a huge crater. Burnside ordered his troops into the crater where they were entrapped and shot down by Confederates along the crater's rim. President Lincoln remarked on this battle: "Only Burnside could have managed such a coup, wringing one last spectacular defeat from the jaws of victory."

Gen. Aleksander Samsonov (1859-1914)

At the start of WWI, the Russian general Samsonov was given command of the Russian Second Army. He had never been a front-line commander, but always a bureaucrat, serving in the rear. Pushing his way into East Prussia, Samsonov had no idea where the Germans were or what he was supposed to do. He completely lost control of his forces, and the Germans easily smashed his disorganized army at the battle of Tannenburg (1914). Samsonov gave up all hope for his army, and rode off to the front to die in battle. Failing to accomplish even that, he committed suicide.

Excerpted from *The Book of Lists* by David Wallechinsky, Irving Wallace, and Amy Wallace (William Morrow & Company, Inc., New York: 1977).

In Sports

In one way or another, professional sports are a part of almost everyone's life. As fans, we're convinced that "our" teams can do no wrong. We feel an almost personal sense of anguish when the New York Yankees let us down on a summer afternoon or the Dallas Cowboys are defeated on a wintry Sunday. Sports fans can be spirited to euphoric highs and plummeted to the depths of despair within the framework of a single game or event. The interested public sees the sporting world as a place where idols and superheroes exist side by side with athletes known as bums, creeps, or by other epithets that could never be printed here.

But like everything else in life, sports provide people with opportunities to stumble. Everyone does it sometimes—remember mighty Casey, whose fabled strike-out so disappointed the fans of Mudville? In the real world, strike-outs or dropped flyballs in the bottom of the ninth have cost many a team a game; hurdles trip runners near the end of their races, there are missed last-second free-throws, double-faulted serves, and six-inch putts that travel only five inches. All of these are understandable lapses; professional sports require a level of proficiency which no human being could

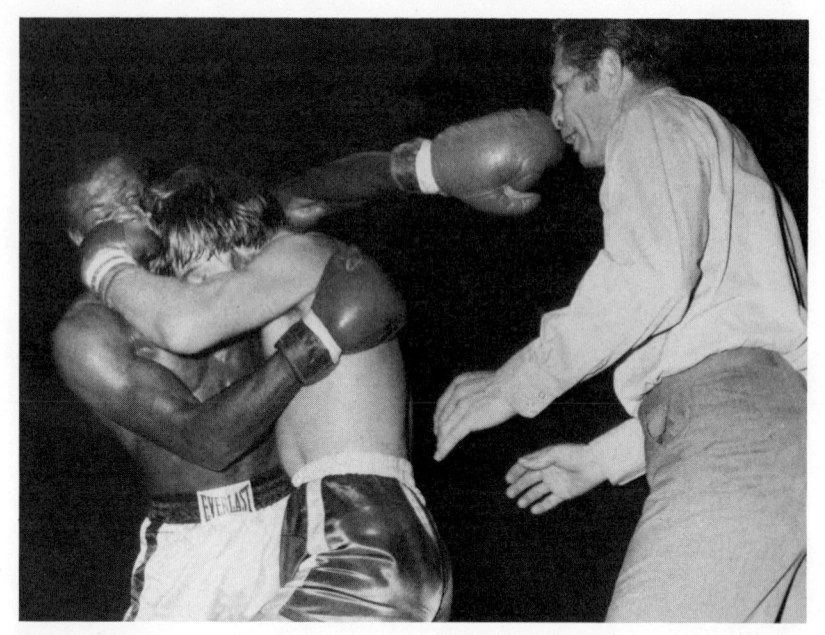

It's not always the athletes who embarrass themselves. Here, referee Lee Sala managed to get his nose a little too close to the action in a match between Willie Cheney (whose glove is flattening Sala's nose) and John Pinney during a 1973 fight in Tampa, Florida.

sustain at all times. But athletes of the past have committed more instructive errors, and it is with these that we are here concerned.

* * * * *

The National Football League was only a few years old in 1924, when a professional player first tried to run the wrong way for a touchdown. In a game between the Chicago Bears and the Columbus Tigers, Bear fullback Oscar Knop leaped to intercept a pass which arced into the air after bouncing off the intended receiver's chest. When Knop grabbed the ball in mid-bounce, he raced off for the goalline—the wrong goalline. Bear back Joey Sternamen yelled at him; Bear tackle Ed Healey sped after him. The entire

Columbus team watched wide-eyed, and some of them began to cheer for Knop. But just before he was to race into the end zone with the dubious distinction of being the first pro football player to score points for the opposing team, Knop's teammate Ed Healey tackled him.

Forty years later, Minnesota Viking defensive end Jim Marshall was not as fortunate. No one caught him. In a game against the San Francisco 49ers, he picked up a fumble and raced sixty yards with it into the wrong end zone. (The 49ers were awarded a safety.)

* * * * *

Germany Schaeffer, an infielder for the Washington Senators in the early 1900s, was a real demon on the basepaths. In one game against the Chicago White Sox, he hit an easy single. While the next batter was up, he raced to second base and slid in—a perfect steal. On the next pitch, he streaked out again—over the same path—and slid back into first base. The White Sox catcher stared down the line in astonishment at Schaeffer, who stood on first base smiling and brushing the dust from his uniform. No one knew what to do. Finally the catcher threw the ball to the first baseman, who stepped on the base and looked imploringly at the umpire. But the umpire shook his head. Schaeffer was safe; he had become the first (and only) major league player to steal first base.

* * * * *

In 1942, the New York Rangers were in desperate need of a goalie. Pickings were slim that year because most able-bodied hockey players in the United States and Canada were in the armed forces fighting World War II. But one of the Rangers' Canadian scouts tracked down a prospect in Saskatchewan and instructed the young man to report immediately to the Rangers training camp. Steve Buzinski was short, skinny, and noticeably bow-legged. Ranger coach Frank Boucher admitted later that when he saw him for the first time as he skated onto the ice at camp, he mistook the new goalie for the boy who cleaned up the ice after team practice. But Buzinski got the job anyway, primarily because there was no one else to take it. Midway through his debut appearance in the National Hockey League, Buzinski was hit in the forehead with a puck. He could feel a little moisture up there, so he took off his goalie mitt and touched the area. When he looked at his fingers, which were smudged with blood, he fainted dead away on the ice. He was revived and managed to finish the game, which the Rangers lost 7-2. In his next appearance, he snagged a fast-flying puck in his mitt and, as goalies so often do, nonchalantly tossed it toward the corner of the rink so a teammate could sweep by and pick it up. Unfortunately, he slung it instead into a corner of the net, giving the Detroit Red Wings one of the twelve goals they scored during that game.

* * * * *

WHAT PRICE GLORY? DEPARTMENT

Bobby Walthour, a six-day bike racing champion, was a little on the clumsy side. As a result of spills and collisions during his bike racing days, he broke his right collarbone twenty-eight times, his left collarbone eighteen times, fractured his ribs thirty-two times, broke six different fingers and one thumb, and accumulated more than a hundred body scars, including sixty stitches in the face and head. During his racing career, he was declared fatally injured six times and pronounced dead twice.

* * * * *

Lefty Gomez of the New York Yankees earned a place in the Major League Baseball Hall of Fame at Cooperstown, New York, for his skill as a pitcher. As a batter, however, he left something to be desired. In one game in 1934, he casually tapped the mud from his cleats with the bat, hitting himself so hard on the ankle that he had to be taken from the field. His ankle swelled to such proportions that he wasn't able to pitch for the next two weeks, missing three turns in the pitching order. (As it was, he won twenty-six games for his team that year anyway.)

* * * * *

The scene was Churchill Downs in Louisville, Kentucky, the date was May 4, 1957. The mint juleps had been downed, "My Old Kentucky Home" had been played, and the horses were at the gate for the eighty-third running of America's most famous horse race, the Kentucky Derby. It promised to be an exciting race; Bold Ruler, the favorite, was being ridden by Eddie Arcaro, the most famous jockey of the day. Two other highly rated horses would be ridden by two of the hottest young jockeys in the business—Willie Hartack would be astride Iron Liege and Gallant Man would be jockeyed by Willie Shoemaker.

The race got under way, and the lead changed hands several times. As the horses thundered into the stretch, Iron Liege was out front. But Gallant Man was coming up fast on the outside under the whip of Willie Shoemaker. From fifth place, he passed horse after horse. Iron Liege tried to hang on to the lead but Gallant Man edged past. With only a little more than a hundred yards to go, Shoemaker suddenly and inexplicably stood up in the stirrups as if the race were over. Gallant Man slowed and Iron Liege moved past him to cross the finish line first. After the race, Shoemaker explained that he had mistaken the one-sixteenth pole for the finish line and thought the race was over.

* * * * *

Fred Merkle of the New York Giants was a fine baseball player, but his name is remembered in the annals of the game primarily for one of the most famous boners ever made on the playing field. It happened in 1908 during a game between the Giants and the Chicago Cubs. The teams were neck and neck in the pennant race that year, and since the victors would represent the National League in the World Series, the outcome of this game was important to both ball clubs. In the last of the ninth inning the score was tied 2-2, but the Giants had runners on first base (Fred Merkle) and on third (Moose McCormick). Al Bridwell lined a single into the outfield, and both base runners took off at the crack of the bat. But when Merkle saw McCormick racing across the plate with the game-winning run, he stopped and trotted off to the dugout. According to the rules, Merkle had to touch second base; otherwise, he could be forced out there. Johnny Evers, Cub second baseman and part of the famous double-play combination Tinker to Evers to Chance, retrieved the ball and stepped on second. The umpire declared Merkle out and therefore, McCormick's run did not count. The game was officially recorded a tie and scheduled to be replayed at the end of the season. When it came time for the play-off, the Giants and the Cubs were tied for first place in the league, so this game would determine which team went on to the World Series. The Giants lost 4-2, and Fred Merkle's boner became a legend in baseball lore.

* * * * *

The fight game has had its share of losers as well, and two certainly deserve mention. In the early part of this century, Babe Malonek sat in his corner before one bout and listened to his manager's last-minute instructions while awaiting the bell for the opening round. "Get right to it," urged his manager. "I want you to race right the hell across the ring and lay into him. Catch him before he can even get his dukes up." The bell clanged. Malonek leaped eagerly from his stool, took two running steps, tripped, and crashed into the floor chin first, knocking himself out. The referee counted to the obligatory ten and the fight was over.

In 1977, Harvey Gartley pranced out of his corner in the first round of a fight, weaving and bobbing for about forty-five seconds.

When he threw his first punch, a wild right that missed, the momentum sent him crashing into the ropes. Gartley toppled to the floor, and when he didn't get up the referee counted him out.

* * * * *

The immortal Lou Gehrig of the New York Yankees lost the home run crown of 1931 because of a blunder. When Gehrig came to bat against the Washington Senators one sunny afternoon, his teammate Lyn Lary was on base. There were two outs, so Lary was on his way as soon as Gehrig hit the ball. He did not see the home run ball sail into the left-centerfield bleachers, and he did not see the ball hit the concrete of the stands and bounce back onto the playing field. As Lary rounded third base, he saw that the coach was giving him no signal and as he looked back he saw the outfielder casually lobbing the ball back to the infield. Lary assumed the ball had been caught for the third out, so instead of continuing on to home plate he trotted over to the Yankee dugout, despite the frenzied screaming of his teammates. Gehrig, oblivious to it all, continued around the bases and crossed home plate, only to be called out for having passed a runner on the basepath. At the end of the season, he had to share the home run crown with fellow Yankee Babe Ruth, both of them having clobbered forty-six four-baggers—at least forty-six that counted.

* * * * *

Northwestern University, a member of the Big Ten, has not in recent years been known for its football prowess in that conference. But back in the mid-1940s they could hold their own—except when they were hell-bent on giving away a game. On November 8, 1947, the gun sounded at the end of a game with Ohio State, and Northwestern was the apparent winner 6-0. Jubilant fans swarmed onto the field, but the referees made them return to the grandstands, explaining that the game was not technically over because on the last play Northwestern had had twelve men on the field. Since Northwestern had been the defensive team on this last play, and since the game could not end on a penalty against the defensive team, officials awarded Ohio State one more play. The Ohio State quarterback faded back and threw a touchdown pass to tie the score. Once again, time had officially run out, but Ohio State was still eligible to try for the game-winning extra point. The kick was blocked, and the fans once again rushed out onto the field. Once again the referees sent them back; Northwestern had been offside on the play. This time the Ohio State place-kicker booted the ball through the uprights to hand Northwestern a 7-6 defeat, fully four minutes after the final gun had sounded.

* * * * *

Hitting a home run is the most exhilarating feat a baseball batter can experience, but the heady sense of victory can totally disconcert a hitter. When Dan O'Leary came to bat for the minor league Point Huron team in a game against a team from Peoria, Illinois, the score was tied. O'Leary laid into a fastball and knocked the ball out of the park, then proceeded to run to third base, to second, to first, and finally back to home plate, crossing it to hear the wide-eyed umpire call him out.

In 1963 the irrepressible Jimmy Piersall, playing then for the New York Mets, hit his 100th career home run and was so delighted with it that he too ran around the bases the wrong way.

* * * * *

In the 1500s, the Aztec Indians of Mexico played a game from which our modern game of basketball is derived. During those earliest days of the sport you were a fool to captain one of the teams, or even to attend a game. The object of the game was to put a rubber ball through a stone ring attached high on the stadium wall. The game ended when the first point was scored, and the scoring player was entitled to the clothing of all the spectators. The losing captain was beheaded.

Some All-time Career Records by the Pros

Baseball
>Most Strikeouts: Mickey Mantle (1,710)
>Most Times Hit by a Pitched Ball: Ronald Hunt (243)
>Most Times Hitting into a Double Play: Hank Aaron (320)
>Most Games Lost by a Pitcher: Cy Young (313)
>Most Runs Allowed by a Pitcher: Red Ruffing (2,117)
>Most Bases on Balls: Early Wynn (1,775)
>Most Batsmen Hit by a Pitcher: Walter Johnson (204)
>Most Home Runs Given Up by a Pitcher: Warren Spahn (434)
>Most Times Caught Stealing: Lou Brock (247)
>Most Errors: Herman Long (shortstop 1,037)

Basketball
>Most Free Throws Missed: Wilt Chamberlain (5,805)
>Most Personal Fouls: Hal Greer (3,855)

Football
>Most Fumbles: Roman Gabriel (95)
>Most Passes Had Intercepted: George Blanda (277)

Hockey
>Most Time Spent in Penalty Box: Ted Lindsay (1,808 minutes)

These eight Major League players share the unpleasant distinction of being the only ballplayers ever to have hit into unassisted triple plays:

Amby McConnell, Boston Red Sox (against the Cleveland Indians, July 19, 1909)

Clarence Mitchell, Brooklyn Dodgers (against the Cleveland Indians, October 10, 1920—a World Series game)

Frank Brower, Cleveland Indians (against the Boston Red Sox, September 14, 1923)

Walter Holke, Philadelphia Phillies (against the Boston Braves, October 6, 1923)

Jim Bottomley, St. Louis Cardinals (against the Pittsburgh Pirates, May 7, 1925)

Paul Waner, Pittsburgh Pirates (against the Chicago Cubs, May 30, 1927)

Homer Summa, Cleveland Indians (against the Detroit Tigers, May 31, 1927)

Joe Azcue, Cleveland Indians (against the Washington Senators, July 30, 1968)

The pros may attract large audiences for their fumbles and strike-outs, but weekend jocks can play the klutz just as competently as their professional counterparts. Almost everybody exercises or competes to some degree, and at some point, the opportunity to slip up is bound to present itself.

You need not participate in a complex sport in order to make a fool of yourself. Jogging, for instance, seems pretty straightforward —put one foot in front of the other, over and over, in rapid progression. Of course, even that can be a problem for clumsy folks, but real klutzes can come up with subtle variations on the theme.

In California recently more than a thousand distance runners were lining up for what promised to be a hotly contested ten-mile race when an automobile on a nearby side street backfired. Race officials and judges watched as more than half of the contestants raced off into the distance.

While jogging is obviously a sport for the active, fishing is for the sedentary. You just sit in a boat, on a pier, or on a riverbank and wait. (We are not talking about those special types who strap themselves into a chair bolted to the deck of an oceangoing boat and spend hours trying to reel in a thousand-pound tuna.)

Let's look at the special bonanza that fishing offers. First of all, you can impale yourself on one of those nifty barbed hooks which are designed *not* to be displaced even by large, voracious sharks once they are embedded in flesh. You can just as easily hook someone else in the boat; your fellow angler's reaction will determine whether this is more or less painful than hooking yourself.

You can fall out of the boat or off the pier. You can drop your new $75 reel into forty feet of water. Then there's the tackle box. All of them have a latch in front (two, if they're of the super-deluxe variety). The latch is there to ensure that the box will be kept securely closed. But invariably, someone in the boat fails to fasten the latch so that when you grab the handle to lift your box it opens like a great mouth, regurgitating every lure, hook, sinker, leader, bobber, snap, scaler, knife, hunk of pork rind, and beer can opener onto the floor of the boat. Picking them all up and replacing each in its proper compartment will take about an hour, plenty of time to let your temper cool before you get down to what you came for—fishing. Of course, when you drop all of these items onto the floor of your aluminum boat, you send sound waves through the water that sound to a fish a little like the blitzkrieg bombing sounded to Londoners during World War II.

If you survive these earlier pitfalls, there's still the chance that you'll lose the stringer of fish it took you all day to accumulate; you may forget to bring it into the boat before starting up the motor and racing across the water for home.

* * * * *

Tennis has become a very popular sport in recent years, even though the waiting lists for most public courts (the free ones) are usually filled through 1986, and the only hours of court-time still available in tennis clubs (the ones that allow you to pay huge amounts of money for the privilege of hitting the little white ball back and forth across a net) are generally from two to three a.m. on alternate Wednesdays. But tennis can be fun and good exercise at the same time. It's fair, too—females can decimate smug males, children can soundly thrash their parents. It is a game in which you can drive to distraction the players on the court next to you by hitting ten consecutive balls into their court or by shouting "Huzzah" every time you score a point.

If you want to get along in the game itself, there are a few rules you need to remember:

Save your cannonball serves for the opponent's court, carefully avoiding the head, neck, and lower back of your doubles partner.

When invited to the Palm Springs Tennis Club, choose your outfit carefully; high-top gym shoes are not *de rigueur* on classy courts.

Never ace your employer 6-0, 6-0, 6-0; you may ace yourself out of a job.

Never attempt to explain the scoring procedure in tennis; you may think you understand it, but you don't.

* * * * *

People generally view the game of golf in one of two classic ways—as an addict views heroin or as a minor irritation that interferes with an otherwise enjoyable walk. But golf is a good sport for the average millionaire who wants to have a good time and get a sunburned face simultaneously. All he needs is a country club membership, a bag of extraordinarily expensive clubs, access to a golf cart so he need not weary himself walking, the ability to drink hard liquor for four consecutive hours in the clubhouse after the rigors of eighteen holes, and the wherewithal to pay off the astronomical gin rummy debts he incurs while drinking in the clubhouse.

Beginners, of course, make many more blunders than the seasoned golfer. They may miss the ball completely, or send it dribbling a few feet up the fairway or onto the green while the preceding foursome is putting. They discover the strange magnetic attraction that exists between the ingredients of a beginner's golf ball and sand or water. They take much longer to play the game (obviously it takes longer to swing a golf club 150 times as you move zig-zag across the course than it does to hit the ball 75 times).

But even the accomplished pros can be klutzy. They can run over a bystander's foot with their golf carts. They can bean a spectator with one of their drives, *a la* Spiro Agnew and Gerald Ford. They can, in a fit of pique, throw golf clubs into eight-foot deep waterholes, at trees, or at other golfers. Such antics are a kind of therapy—at least that's how golfers see it. We knew one man—

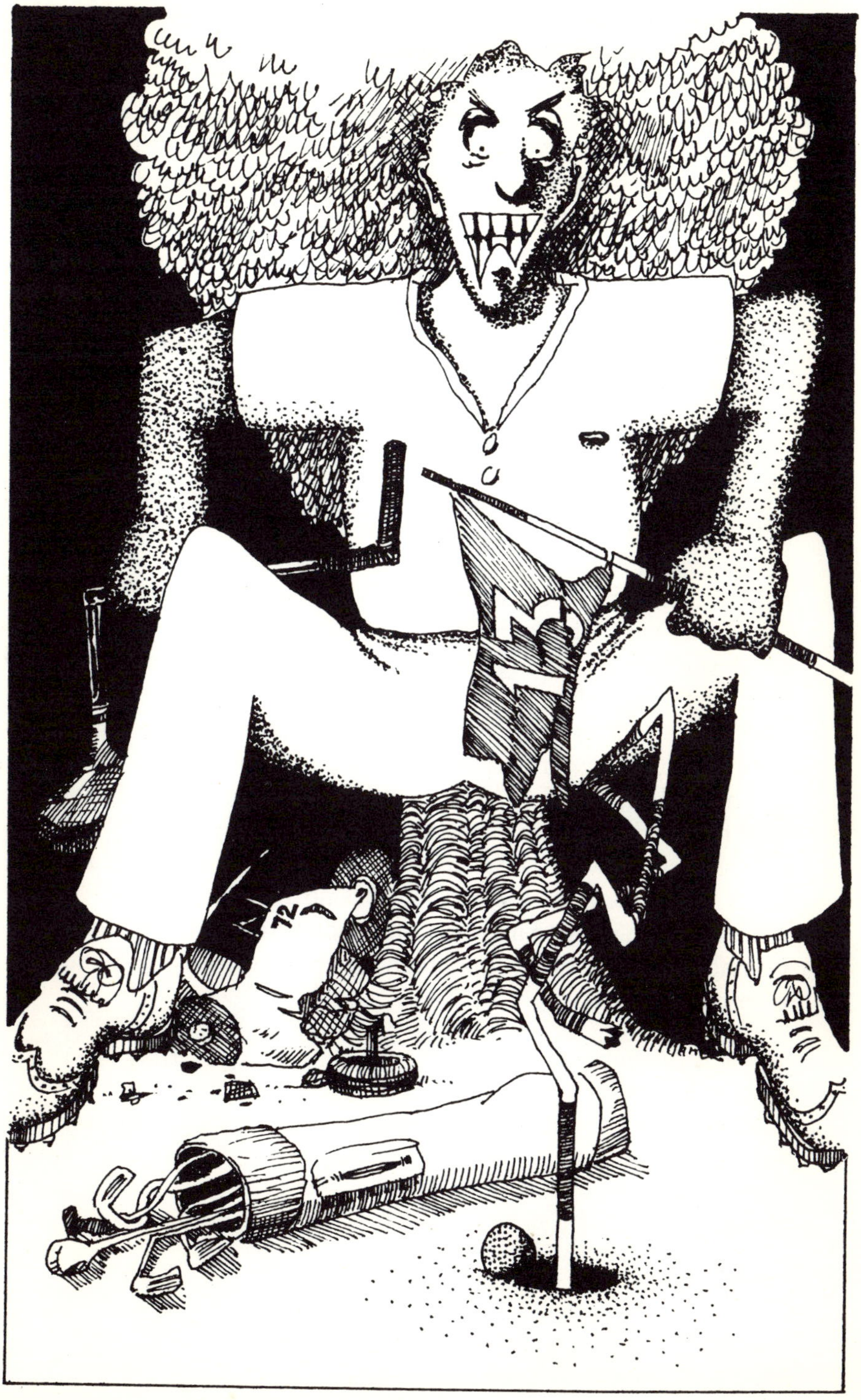
72

and this is a true story—who stood in a sandtrap on the fifth hole of the Fort Myers Country Club in Florida and "therapeutically" slung his sand wedge into the air. He watched, astonished, as it passed across a heavily traveled roadway, neatly slipping between and over many cars before dropping into a crowded swimming pool at a motel across the street. At another time on that same hole, it is rumored that the same fellow buried his putter to the grip in a fit of anger.

A doctor at the Congressional Country Club in Bethesda, Maryland, once bludgeoned a Canada goose to death with his putter because its honking allegedly disturbed his putting on the seventeenth green. He had to pay a fine; Canadian geese are protected by the Migratory Bird Treaty Act, a federal law.

IF AT FIRST YOU DON'T SUCCEED DEPARTMENT

In 1912, a young woman golfer totted up 166 strokes on a 130-yard hole in a ladies tournament at Shawnee-on-Delaware, Pennsylvania. It was the sixteenth hole and she needed just under two hours to send the ball rolling into the cup. As it happened, she had hit her tee shot into the Binniekill River. But the ball floated, and when she saw it bobbing on the water she commandeered a rowboat and assigned her husband to the oars. She stood in the bow and took a vicious swing each time they approached the ball. This went on for some time as they pursued the ball, which was being carried with the current. After a number of swipes—her husband kept track for her—she finally managed to beach the ball 1½ miles downstream. Now she was separated from the golf course by a small forest. But undaunted she began whacking the ball through the trees until finally it emerged from that stupendous rough. From there she was able to chip it onto the green and putt out, only 162 strokes over par.

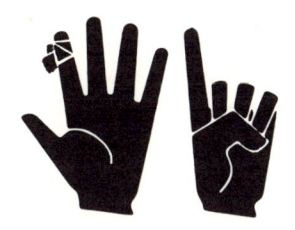

Our Way With Words

Ever since those alleged first words were uttered—"Madam, I'm Adam"—language has proven itself a superb vehicle for getting us into trouble, embarrassing ourselves publicly, and giving us the opportunity to reveal those personal characteristics that we might prefer to keep under wraps.

- It helps us prove that we're on the ball: "Nice to have met you, Jim," we smile after being introduced—to John.
- It showcases our sincerity: "Joe, I want you to meet my good friend . . ." We grope in vain for the name of that "good" friend."
- And it's great for highlighting tact: "Jane, I really like that dress you're wearing; I admired it at our last party."

At other times, we manage to sound just plain stupid:
"Correct me if I'm right."
"It was so dark you couldn't see your face in front of you."
"If he were alive today, he'd turn over in his grave."
"We only want those of you who are here to answer 'present'."

"I can't wait to get there, even if I never do."

"It's good to see your voice."

Perhaps a neighbor tells us that a mutual acquaintance has recently died of a heart attack. We respond, "Well, thank God it wasn't something worse." Then we must spend the rest of the evening explaining that a quick, painless death seems preferable to some protracted torture like cancer or leprosy or jungle rot.

Some instances by their very nature prompt us to founder. When we visit the family or loved ones at a funeral, the bereaved thanks us for coming to pay our respects. What do we say? Invariably something like "I wouldn't have missed it for the world." Or, "It's great to be here." Or, "I'm sure glad I had the chance to come."

* * * * *

You don't need to say the wrong thing to put your foot in your mouth—you can achieve the same effect by saying the right thing in the wrong way. One linguistic trailblazer of this variety was the Reverend William A. Spooner (1844-1930), dean of New College at Oxford, England. His specialty bears his name, a figure of speech called the *spoonerism*. Dictionaries define this affliction as "a slip of the tongue whereby initial or other sounds of words are accidentally transposed." The Reverend Mr. Spooner pepped up the English language with his unintentional slips—often, what he said made more sense than what he had intended to say:

"The queer old dean" ("The dear old queen")

"I have a half-warmed fish in my mind" ("I have a half-formed wish in my mind")

"It is kisstumary to cuss the bride" ("It is customary to kiss the bride")

"Kinquering congs their titles take" ("Conquering kings their titles take")

"You have deliberately tasted two worms and you can leave Oxford by the town drain" ("You have deliberately wasted two terms and you can leave Oxford by the noon train").

* * * * *

President Warren G. Harding had a unique way with words, expressing himself in a way that often baffled even the most sagacious of his colleagues. Stephen Pile celebrates Harding in his *Book of Historic Failures*, suggesting that the president may have been the world's worst speech writer.

"Warren Gamaliel Harding wrote his own speeches while president of the United States in the 1920s and people queued up to pay tribute.

H. L. Mencken said: 'He writes the worst English that I have ever encountered. It is so bad that a sort of grandeur creeps into it.'

When Harding died, e. e. cummings said: 'The only man, woman or child who wrote a simple declarative sentence with seven grammatical errors is dead.'

Here is a rewarding sample of the man's style:

'I would like the government to do all it can to mitigate, then, in understanding, in mutuality of interest, in concern for the common good, our tasks will be solved.'"

If Warren G. Harding was linguistically inept on the national level of government in the United States, Mayor Richard J. Daley of Chicago was uniquely eloquent on the local level. Daley, called king-maker by many and certainly one of the most influential mayors in the history of the United States, had a penchant for saying things he did not mean. For example:

"Today we have reached a new platitude of success."

"Don't confuse me with the facts."

In reference to the rioting and police violence at the Democratic National Convention in Chicago in 1968: "Gentlemen, get it straight for once and for all. The policeman is not there to create disorder. The policeman is there to preserve disorder."

Regarding that same illustrious period in the American story: "I don't think there is any more division today than there was in the Civil War or any other time in our history."

"What keeps people apart is their inability to get together."

"The Bears (Chicago's professional football team) have demonsplayed the will to win."

Warren G. Harding

And upon the opening of the refurbished stadium known as Soldier Field, among the many things the mayor mentioned he could now look forward to were "aquatic events." People began to wonder whether he meant *equestrian* events or whether he indeed intended to flood the outdoor stadium.

* * * * *

Even our eminent diplomats, who base their careers on the strategic use of tact, have provided a dilly or two. For example, Warren Austin, the U.S. Ambassador to the United Nations during Israel's War for Independence in 1948, chided the warring Arabs and Jews to "resolve their differences like good Christians."

* * * * *

Broadcasters on radio and television are as human as the rest of us. Certainly many of them make average bloopers from time to time, or become embarrassingly tongue-tied, or abuse the language in their own special ways. Like this famous gentleman, as recorded for posterity in *Reader's Digest:*

> "Dizzy Dean, former star pitcher for the St. Louis Cardinals, was a huge success as a television broadcaster of baseball games, partly because of the innovations he has made in our language. 'He slud into third' was the first much-publicized departure. Later he varied 'slud' with 'slood,' and then one afternoon came up with, 'The trouble with them boys is they ain't got enough spart.' Pressed for an explanation of this, he obliged: 'Spart is pretty much the same as fight or pep or gumption. Like the *Spart of St. Louis,* the plane Lindbergh flowed to Europe in.'"

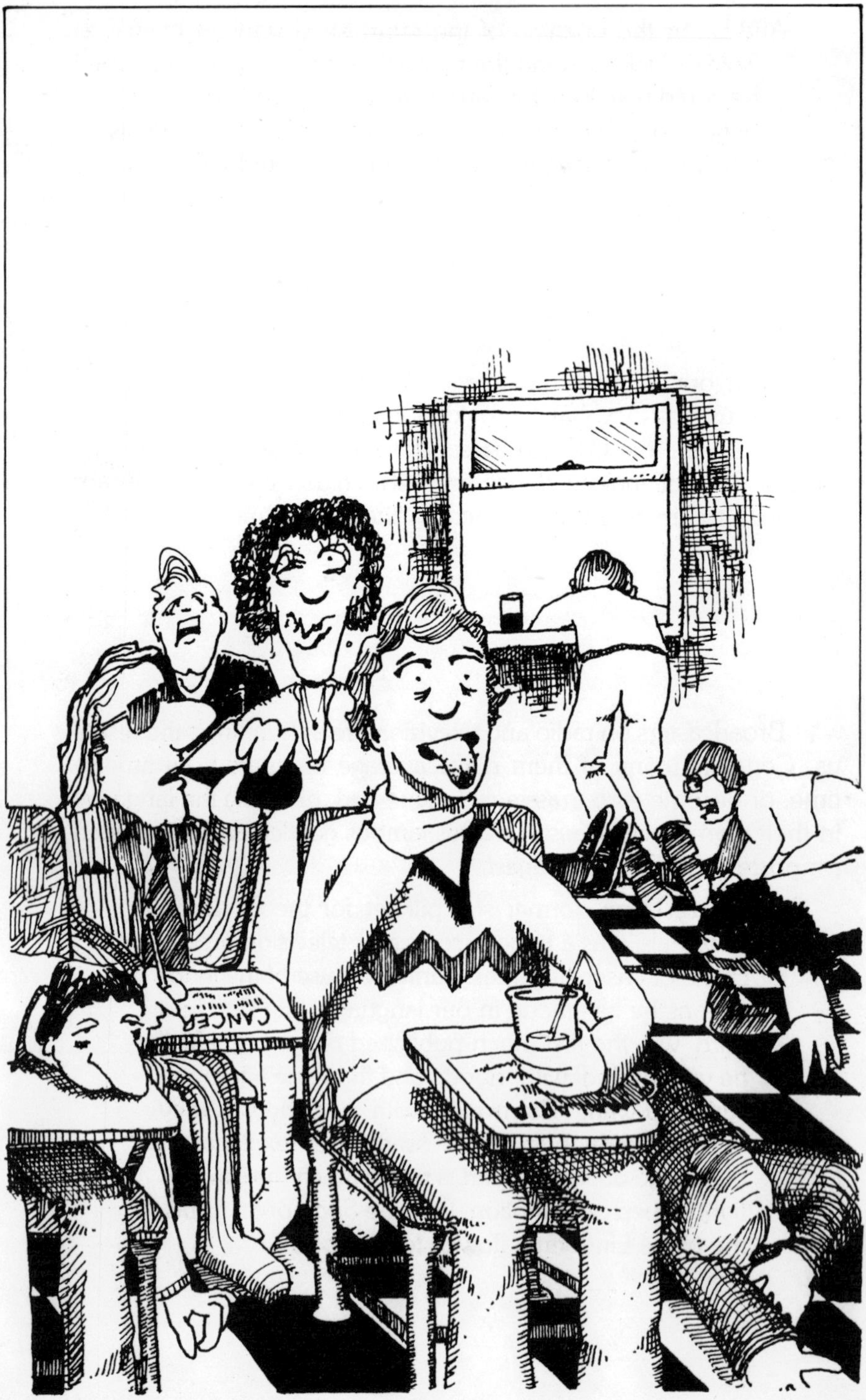
CANCER

Betty Furness, longtime spokesperson for various products on television, once advised sagely on a live commercial: "Try your Westinghoush wather with a full load on."

Another classic from the famous collection *Pardon My Blooper* was offered by the announcer who provided this information: "And now, Nelson Eddy sings 'While My Lady Sleeps' with the men's chorus."

* * * * *

Magazines and other periodicals fare not a whole lot better.

From *Ladies Home Journal*, this cosmopolitan observation: "But to the debutante who arrived too late for the last flaring skyrocket, it was thrilling enough just to see the familiar surroundings transformed into exotic old Vienna, with painted gondolas afloat on mock canals."

From *Business Week*, in an article on how marriage affects the economy and business in general: "It should be at least a year or two before the bulge appears in marriage figures."

From *True Romance:* "I stared soberly into my mirror that night as I combed my lone straight hair. I knew I was not very pretty."

From *Sutton Island, Maine:* "Another rare visitor was an Arctic Three-toed Woodpecker which was attracted by the extensive burnt-over area in the center of the island and which took 200 Civilian Conservation Corps young men luckily stationed at Southwest Harbor to extinguish."

From the *Bulletin of the Medical University of South Carolina:* "Internal Medicine—Richland Memorial Hospital (Columbia) 22 credit hours. Students will be introduced to the principles and practice of internal medicine on a level that is as advanced as each can individually handle. They will be exposed to a variety of disease conditions and will die."

From the *Tourist Information Guide, Hong Kong:* "Drums beat loudly, cymbals clash, the wind and other instruments are played full blast. For sheer magnificence of spectacle, Chinese operas are unbearable."

The newspapers have transformed typographical errors into an art form:

> From the San Angelo (Texas) *Standard:* "*Correction*—First place winner of the First Late St. Valentine's Massacre Chili Cookoff last weekend at Circle Bar Truck Corral near Ozona was the Orehouse Chili team of San Antonio rather than the Whorehouse Chili Team as was inadvertently announced in the Sunday and Monday editions of the Standard Times. The S-T regrets the error and any embarrassment it may have caused members of the chili team."

They have also offered some arresting turns of phrase:

> From the Bayonne (New Jersey) *Times:* "Ten percent of everything American women put into Maidenform bras each year goes for advertising."

> From the *Rocky Mountain News* (Denver): "She looked like the belle of a court ball with the gown and her hair piled high on her head."

> From the Ketchikan (Alaska) *Progressive Alaskan*, an ad: "Spend your Saturday nights at the Hacienda and your Sunday mornings in bed with a Progressive Alaskan."

From the Boston *Herald-American*, "Dear Abby" column:

> DEAR ABBY: A few years ago you ran an article about a woman who never cooked her own Thanksgiving or Christmas dinner. Instead, she went to her mother's or her mother-in-law's. She wrote to say that she wishes now that she had done her own holiday dinners.
>
> That letter was terrific. If you could publish it again, it would be a great help to a lot of people.
>
> I am a grandmother who wishes my married children would cook their own holiday dinners and invite me as a guest.
>
> PAID MY DUES

DEAR PAID: It wasn't hard to find, and here it is:

DEAR ABBY: No names please. If anyone knew I wrote this I'd die of embarrassment. What is the difference between a mule, a donkey, and a jackass?

And we cannot neglect Abby's sister Ann Landers. From the San Juan (Puerto Rico) *Star:*

"Ann Landers will be glad to help you with your parents. Send them to her in care of this newspaper, enclosing a stamped, self-addressed envelope."

The newspapers also offer some headline highlights:

From the Philadelphia *Bulletin:* "Maker of Gases Expects to Expand"

From the Springfield (Massachusetts) *Union:* "Escaped Leopard Believed Spotted"

From the Canton (Ohio) *Repository:* "Key Witness Takes Fifth in Liquor Probe"

Coping

The only way to ensure that we will never do anything klutzy is to take care that we never do anything or say anything at all. But even the laziest, least ambitious person has to go out on a limb and exert some energy from time to time. To live with our humanity and the accompanying faults and failings, we must learn to *cope*.

To cope with our human frailty, we have to be able to laugh at mistakes and blunders. We have to see the humor (quietly, of course) when others act like klutzes. Most important, we must learn to laugh at ourselves.

Knowing what to expect can help—for example, at hearth and home. If your spouse and your children always find great merriment in your moments of disgrace, you will find that *expecting* their occasional taunts and shrieks of laughter makes them easier to bear.

We should treat our klutzy moments with cultivated indifference. We must apply the old principle that football coaches have offered to athletes for decades (whether they have a slight bruise or a caved-in chest)—"Shake it off." When a loved one or a friend reminds us of our latest boner, we need only chuckle with an air of superiority, perhaps reminding our tormentor of the last thing he or she did that was worth a good laugh. If an enemy reminds us of our human flaws, we need not retaliate with a barrage of violence, hate letters, obscene telephone calls, catcalls, or scabrous remarks about the person's heritage. One of these will suffice. Or better, we can just ignore the slob with a finely developed aura of superiority because *we* understand the basic truth of humanity.

We should always approach things such as home repairs, family outings, and leisure-time sports with care and respect for the inherent pitfalls. None of us is Heloise or Mr. Fix-it or Arnie Palmer or Chris Evert, and it helps to remember that.

If we understand that inanimate objects are man's and woman's natural enemies, that they are put on this earth to harass us, sometimes injure us, often frustrate us, and usually annoy us, we will have won half the battle. On the other hand, if we look upon the people we deal with in normal circumstances as human, trouble-prone beings whose basic task in life, like ours, is to cope, we may turn out to be downright charitable.

In the end, all we can do is try our best, accept the bad and glory in the good. There's nothing wrong with a little swearing, a good long cry, or a brief respite at the liquor cabinet if these will help ease the trauma of coping.

After all, we're only human.